VIRGINIA

Past and Present

Jason Porterfield

rosen publishing's
rosen
central®

New York

Published in 2010 by The Rosen Publishing Group, Inc.
29 East 21st Street, New York, NY 10010

First Edition

Library of Congress Cataloging-in-Publication Data

Porterfield, Jason.
Virginia: past and present / Jason Porterfield.—1st ed.
    p. cm.—(The United States: past and present)
Includes bibliographical references and index.
ISBN-13: 978-1-4358-5289-1 (library binding)
ISBN-13: 978-1-4358-5576-2 (pbk)
ISBN-13: 978-1-4358-5577-9 (6 pack)
1. Virginia—History—Juvenile literature. I. Title.
F226.3.P67 2009
975.5—dc22

2008054403

Manufactured in the United States of America

On the cover: Top left: Settlers trade with Native Americans at the Jamestown settlement in 1609. Jamestown was the first permanent English settlement in North America. Top right: A crowd attends a christening ceremony, held in April 2007, for a newly launched nuclear submarine in Newport News. Bottom: Ponies surge across the Assateague Channel during the annual Chincoteague Pony Swim. The event often features more than two hundred ponies.

Contents

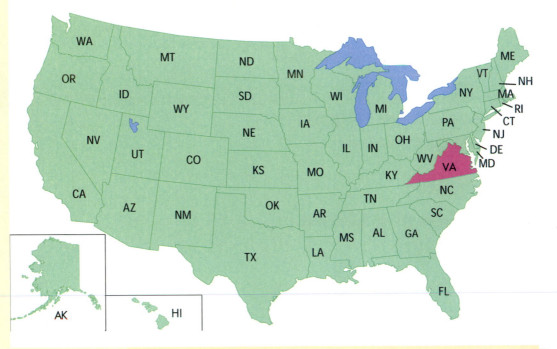

Virginia is located near the center of the Atlantic coast. The nation's capital, Washington, D.C., is just across the Potomac River.

Introduction

By 1781, the thirteen colonies that would eventually become the United States had been fighting the Revolutionary War against England for nearly six years. The war often looked hopeless for the colonies and their ragtag Continental army, led by Virginian George Washington. That spring, however, Washington managed to corner a British army led by General Charles Cornwallis near Yorktown, located along Virginia's coast. With the help of French ships, Washington defeated Cornwallis and captured his army.

Cornwallis's surrender essentially marked the end of the Revolutionary War. It also signified the beginning of a new country and Virginia's role in shaping it. Virginia had been at the forefront of the country's history since 1607, when European settlers established the Jamestown colony along the Atlantic coast.

Washington and other Virginians help establish the new nation. Decades later, Virginia's state capital, Richmond, was chosen as the capital of the Confederate States of America at the onset of the American Civil War because of the state's historic importance.

Today, Virginia is home to more than seven million people. Though the state is deeply connected to its rich history and traditions, it is now also home to an expanding technology industry. Even as Virginians look to the future, however, the many parks and historic sites throughout the state continue to link them to the country's early formation and growth.

Chapter 1

THE GEOGRAPHY OF VIRGINIA

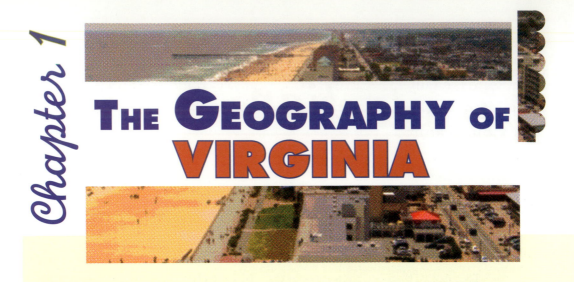

When Europeans first colonized Virginia in the early seventeenth century, they found a land of extremes. They initially settled on the flat eastern coastland, dominated by rivers, swamps, islands, and peninsulas along the Chesapeake Bay. Farther inland, the country-side turned into rolling hills and forests, while the colony's western edge was defined by the rugged Appalachian Mountains. Throughout much of the seventeenth and eighteenth centuries, the Appalachians formed the western boundary of the American colonies and, later, the United States. Few white settlers strayed beyond these mountains and ventured into the vast frontier stretching out for thousands of miles behind them.

Virginia ranks thirty-fifth in total land area among all fifty states, with 42,326 square miles (109,390 square kilometers). The state has a long southern border that it shares with Tennessee and North Carolina, narrowing to the northeast. Its borders form an elongated triangle shape with Kentucky and West Virginia to the west and Maryland and Washington, D.C., to the north. The state's eastern border is made up of 112 miles (180 km) of ocean coastline. It is considered one of the Mid-Atlantic states because of its location near the center of the Atlantic coast.

The state is easily divided into three distinct regions: the Tidewater, the Piedmont, and the Ridge and Valley. Each of these regions reflects a geographic feature of the state.

The Tidewater

The Tidewater is the easternmost part of the state. This low-lying region is dominated by rivers and peninsulas, particularly near the coast. Rivers and creeks in the eastern part of the state drain into the Atlantic Ocean. They carve long, narrow peninsulas—called necks—into the landscape as they merge with the region's larger rivers.

The rivers, islands, and peninsulas give the state 3,315 miles (5,335 km) of shoreline. Most of this shoreline consists of estuaries—places where ocean water mixes with freshwater from the rivers during high tide—along the Chesapeake Bay. Many brackish (salty) swamps have formed around these estuaries. The largest is the Dismal Swamp, a 63,000-acre (255 sq km) marsh that extends south into North Carolina. Lake Drummond, one of only two naturally occurring freshwater lakes in the state, is located in the swamp.

Four main rivers run through the Tidewater: the Potomac, the Rappahannock, the James, and the York. The Potomac forms the state's border with Maryland and Washington, D.C. The Potomac River to the north and the Rappahannock River to the south form the first of three major mainland peninsulas, the Northern Neck. The second, the Middle Neck, lies between the Rappahannock and the York rivers. The Lower Peninsula is formed by the York and James rivers.

The most notable of Virginia's peninsulas is the Delmarva Peninsula, sometimes called the Eastern Shore (its name is a combination of Delaware, Maryland, and Virginia). The Delmarva Peninsula extends

A kayaker paddles off a series of waterfalls on the Potomac River. The Potomac is the northernmost river in Virginia.

south from Maryland and forms part of Maryland and Delaware. It is separated from Virginia's mainland by the Chesapeake Bay, the largest bay in the United States and one of the largest in the world.

The bay is about 200 miles (322 km) long and extends from the city of Virginia Beach to Havre de Grace, Maryland. At its narrowest point, near Aberdeen, Maryland, the bay is 3.4 miles (5.5 km) wide. Its widest point is near the mouth of the Potomac River, where it's about 35 miles (56 km) wide. The bay supports more than 3,600 species of fish, plants, and animals, including 173 species of shellfish and 29 species of waterfowl. The bay has long been an important part of the state's economy, particularly to the Tidewater's fishing industry.

South of the Chesapeake Bay, the James River joins with two smaller rivers, the Elizabeth and the Nansemond, to form a large estuary called Hampton Roads. The cities that sprang up around Hampton Roads—including Norfolk, Hampton, Newport News, and Portsmouth—together form one of the busiest ports in the world.

The Piedmont

The Piedmont region covers the central part of the state. The region's eastern boundaries are easily marked by a sudden change in the landscape called the Fall Line. This is a rock ridge that is significantly higher than the Tidewater region. The rivers that flow east from the mountains—such as the Potomac, York, James, and Rappahannock—cascade over waterfalls and rapids at this ridge. Cities like Richmond, Fredericksburg, and Alexandria formed along the fall line because ships couldn't travel farther west up the rivers.

The land forms a plateau that gradually rises to the west of the Fall Line, from an elevation of 300 feet (91 meters) at the line itself to about 1,200 feet (366 m) on the Piedmont's western side. The Piedmont extends from the North Carolina border all the way to the outskirts of Washington, D.C. Though hilly, the region's soil is fertile and has long been used as farmland. Agriculture remains an important industry in the region, even as the suburbs of Washington, D.C., extend into the northern part of the Piedmont. Many forests of pines and hardwoods, such as oak and maple, also cover the hills.

McAfee Knob, located on Catawba Mountain in southwestern Virginia, is one of the most photographed points along the Appalachian Trail.

The Ridge and Valley Region

The Ridge and Valley region consists of a series of mountain ranges that form part of the ancient Appalachian Mountain system, including the Blue Ridge and Allegheny mountain ranges. The Blue Ridge range, the easternmost of Virginia's mountain ranges, gets its name from the blue-green tinge that the mountains appear to have from a distance. Virginia's highest point, Mount Rogers (5,729 feet; 1,746 m), is in the southern part of the Blue Ridge.

The Allegheny Mountains are west of the Blue Ridge. Both ranges are marked by rivers, caves, and rock formations either carved by running water or shaped as the mountains eroded. A large portion of the Appalachian Trail—a 2,175-mile (3,500 km) long footpath stretching from Georgia to Maine—passes through both ranges.

A fertile valley called the Valley of Virginia separates the Allegheny and Blue Ridge mountains. The valley actually consists of several smaller valleys, often defined by the rivers that helped form them. The Shenandoah Valley to the north, drained by the Shenandoah River, is the largest of these valleys. The Shenandoah Valley was once the floor of a shallow sea, and many strange rock formations—called chimneys—formed when the sea receded. Natural Bridge, a massive natural limestone arch 215 feet (66 m) high and 90 feet (27 m) across, is one of the most famous formations in the valley.

The Ridge and Valley region is mostly rural. Much of it is also forested. Two huge national forests, the Jefferson National Forest and the Washington National Forest, combine to take up about 1.8 million acres (7,284 sq km), crossing over into a handful of counties in Kentucky and West Virginia. The largest city is Roanoke, with about ninety-four thousand residents. Several college towns, such as Blacksburg, Harrisonburg, and Lexington, are also scattered throughout the region.

Climate

Virginia has a moderate climate. Along the coast, days are often warm and sunny. Normal temperatures can range from about 50 degrees Fahrenheit (10 degrees Celsius) in the winter to the upper 90s (higher than 35°C) throughout much of the summer. Norfolk's

The Chincoteague Ponies

Assateague Island is a small barrier island just off the coast of the Delmarva Peninsula. As the core of the Assateague Island National Seashore, the island is protected and home to many species of plants and animals. The most famous of these animals are the island's wild ponies. These ponies are believed to be the descendents of survivors of a Spanish shipwreck more than three hundred years ago. Others believe they are descended from domesticated ponies that were released by seventeenth-century colonists to avoid paying taxes on them to the English government.

Today, more ponies are born than the island can support. For decades, people living in nearby communities have herded the young ponies and made them swim across a narrow channel to nearby Chincoteague Island for auction. Those that are not sold swim back to Assateague Island. While some people criticize the practice, others point out that if the ponies are not removed from the island, its ecosystem could collapse.

Wild ponies live on the islands off Virginia's eastern shore. An annual roundup keeps the population in check.

average temperature ranges from about 47°F (8°C) in January to about 86°F (30°C) in July. Around the Washington, D.C., area, temperatures tend to be hotter and more humid. The city was built on a swamp, and the area remains very damp. In the mountains, the weather tends to be dryer and cooler than in the Piedmont and Tidewater. The heavy forests in the Ridge and Valley region are widely known for their spectacular autumn foliage as the leaves change color.

Rainfall and snowfall in the state are moderate. Even in the mountains, annual snowfall rarely totals more than 2 to 3 feet (0.61 to 0.91 m). There are exceptions, however, such as the blizzards that, though rare, can blow across the mountains or the occasional hurricane barreling inland from the coast.

The Chesapeake Bay is home to many species of fish and other sea life, including Virginia's famous and sought-after crabs.

Plants and Animals

When English colonists landed in Virginia in 1607, they found forests of pines, oak, ash, and walnut. They also discovered open meadows where Native Americans harvested maize—a type of corn—and tobacco. Red deer and fallow deer lived in the meadows, as did rabbits, woodchucks, and foxes. Farther west, the forests grew more dense and were home to raccoons, black bears, bobcats, opossums, and wild turkeys.

Today, about half of Virginia is still covered by forest. It remains inhabited by many of the animals that colonists found when they first arrived, including black bears and bobcats. Wild ponies can be found on the islands along the eastern shore. They're believed to be descendents of horses that swam to the islands from shipwrecks during the seventeenth and eighteenth centuries. The forests are also home to many birds, such as orioles, cardinals, wild turkeys, grouse, and hummingbirds. Along the shore there is an even greater diversity of birds like snow geese, pelicans, ducks, falcons, herons, and bald eagles.

Unfortunately, pollution and overfishing have damaged populations of many fish and other marine life forms, while habitat destruction along the coast has affected nesting grounds for birds. However, the Chesapeake Bay still has populations of crabs and oysters, as well as fish, sharks, and dolphins.

Both poisonous and nonpoisonous snakes can be found in Virginia. Several species of rattlesnakes can be found throughout the state. Copperheads are common in forested regions, and the venomous cottonmouth is found in the Dismal Swamp region. Nonpoisonous snakes include garter snakes, black racers, and king snakes.

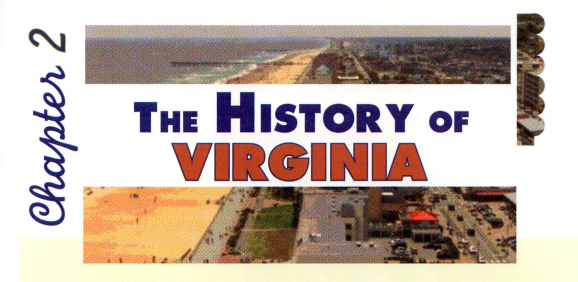

Chapter 2

THE HISTORY OF VIRGINIA

After several unsuccessful attempts to establish colonies in North America, England's King James I gave the territory that is now Virginia to a group of investors called the Virginia Company in 1606. He granted them this charter on the condition that company members explore the land and build a settlement. The first European settlers landed at what is now Virginia Beach in 1607. The colonists had hoped to find valuable products like gold, gems, and spices in the new colony. Instead, they found forests and open meadows teeming with wildlife. Farther up the coast, they established Jamestown, the first permanent English settlement in North America.

Life in Early Jamestown

The colonists knew very little about frontier life, and the settlement was almost wiped out in its early years by the combination of disease, a long drought, and a series of harsh winters. During the winter of 1609–1610, about 435 out of 500 colonists died of disease and starvation as the food supply ran low.

Without the help of the Powhatan tribe and the arrival of more settlers and supplies the following spring, the settlement would have been abandoned. The Powhatan taught settlers how to grow corn

Historical re-enactors demonstrate routines of daily life in Virginia's Jamestown settlement. Jamestown was England's first successful colony in North America.

and other crops, and the colonists themselves discovered that the region's soil was very good for growing tobacco. The crop quickly became the colony's first profitable export to England.

Relations with the Powhatan became strained as the settlement expanded and colonists encroached on the tribe's lands. In one famous incident, John Smith, one of the colony's leaders, was captured by the Powhatan. Smith later reported that he was tied to rocks and was about to be killed when Chief Powhatan's daughter Matoaka—nicknamed Pocahontas, meaning "playful one"—convinced the chief to spare his life.

English soldiers eventually forced many of the Powhatan and other tribes to abandon their lands and move west. The colonists themselves also began moving west in search of new farmland, with some moving into the Piedmont by the 1650s. By the late 1700s, much of Virginia's Native American population had either died of diseases brought over by colonists or been driven out of the state.

In 1619, the colony established a representative government. It consisted of an upper house of men appointed by the governor (the

The tobacco-based economy of early Virginia depended on slave labor. By 1790, slaves made up about 40 percent of Virginia's population.

Governor's Council) and a lower house of elected representatives called the House of Burgesses.

The Introduction of Slavery

While the colonists were taking their first steps toward democracy, they also began moving toward the shameful practice of slavery. In 1619, the same year Virginia's representative government was established, a Dutch slave ship brought twenty Africans to the colony. They came as indentured servants, meaning that they were set free

17

PAST AND PRESENT

Virginia's First Residents

Virginia's first permanent residents were long believed to have been Native Americans who settled in the region about four thousand years ago. The powerful Powhatan and Susquehanna tribes lived in the Tidewater region, the Monacan and Manahoac lived in the central part of the state, and the Cherokee controlled the west. However, recent discoveries of stone tools near the town of Saltville have led some anthropologists to believe that Native Americans may have settled the region more than fourteen thousand years ago.

Today, eight tribes (including the Monacan) call Virginia home, and the state has two reservations. About 2,500 people are registered as tribe members, and 15,000 people living in Virginia are believed to be of Native American ancestry.

According to legend, intervention by Pocahontas of the Powhatan tribe saved the life of early colonial explorer John Smith.

once they worked off the cost of their passage to Virginia. As tobacco farmers became more successful, however, they began enslaving Africans to work on their plantations. In 1661, Virginia's House of Burgesses wrote the first law in the American colonies to allow slavery. Unlike indentured servants, slaves were not given the opportunity to work toward their eventual freedom.

The slave population in Virginia grew quickly. Fearful of the possibility of a slave rebellion, colonists passed laws further restricting the freedom of slaves. While some leaders in Virginia occasionally questioned the morality of slavery, nothing was done to end the practice in the American South until slavery was forcibly abolished by President Abraham Lincoln during the Civil War.

Breaking from England

By the middle of the seventeenth century, Virginia was a prosperous colony, thanks to the tobacco crop. More colonists moved into the state, and the land east of the Fall Line started getting crowded. A growing number of colonists, particularly immigrants from France, Germany, Scotland, and Ireland, settled in the Piedmont. At times, these western colonists found themselves at odds with the colonial government in Jamestown.

England saw its American colonies as a source of raw materials and wealth that served the kingdom. The colonists, however, had come to chafe under English rule and began to crave greater liberty and autonomy (self-governance). In response, the English government began limiting the independence of the colonies. For example, it forbade settlers from moving into lands once held by the French, where they would be harder to govern and their activities more difficult to monitor.

England also imposed new and expensive taxes on the colonies. Many leaders and thinkers in Virginia began meeting to talk about issues like the Stamp Act, a much-hated tax that the English government forced them to pay for every official document that was drafted.

In 1774, the king's governor of Virginia forced the House of Burgesses to close, ending colonists' participation in the government of the colony. Colonists in Virginia, such as Patrick Henry, Thomas Jefferson, and George Mason, quickly became some of the most vocal advocates for forming a new country independent of England. When the thirteen

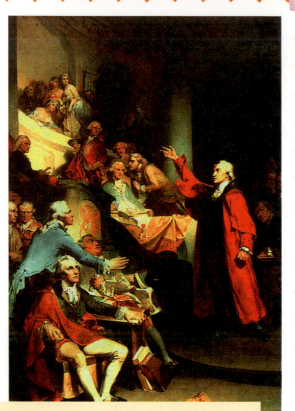

Addressing the House of Burgesses, Patrick Henry helped rouse the revolutionary spirit among his fellow Virginians with his fiery speeches.

colonies went to war with England in 1775, Virginian George Washington took command of the Continental army, while Thomas Jefferson wrote the Declaration of Independence in 1776. Though little of the war was actually fought in Virginia, the war's last battle took place at coastal Yorktown in 1781.

Virginians played a major role in the war's aftermath. James Madison wrote the U.S. Constitution in 1787, using Virginia's own constitution as a model. George Washington was elected the first U.S. president. The former governor of Virginia, Thomas Jefferson, was Washington's secretary of state before being elected himself to serve as the nation's third president. Other Virginians followed in the footsteps of Washington and Jefferson to become president in the country's early years, including James Madison.

Rising Tensions

As the new country came together, it became clear that major differences existed between the Northern states and the Southern states. Southern states like Virginia had economies based largely on agriculture. These states allowed slavery and had large slave populations. Slavery was banned in the Northern states, where the economy was based more on manufacturing and trade. During the nineteenth century, tensions between the North and the South grew over the legality and morality of slavery.

In October 1859, an abolitionist named John Brown and a group of his followers seized a federal arsenal at the small Virginia town of Harpers Ferry. They intended to use the weapons stored there to begin a massive slave rebellion. Brown's plan failed and he was executed, but the incident foreshadowed a greater storm gathering on the horizon.

The Civil War

After Abraham Lincoln was elected president in 1860, several Southern states seceded to form the Confederate States of America. They feared Lincoln would abolish slavery. Virginia remained part of the United States until April 1861, when Confederate troops began the Civil War by firing on federal soldiers at Fort Sumter, South Carolina. At that point, Virginia also left the Union, and the Confederate capital was moved to Richmond.

The Civil War lasted four years and claimed more than 800,000 lives. More Civil War battles were fought in Virginia than in any other state, and the state's farms, towns, and cities suffered greatly at the hands of the two clashing armies. The state even lost territory, as many western counties separated from the state to form West Virginia in 1862. By the time Confederate general Robert E. Lee, a Virginian, surrendered his army to Union general Ulysses S. Grant at the tiny Virginia town of Appomattox Courthouse in April 1865, Richmond had been virtually leveled.

Recovery and Progress

Here, General Lee, dressed in the gray uniform of the Confederacy, surrenders to General Grant at Appomattox Courthouse.

Virginia's recovery from the Civil War was a slow process. Many of the state's factories and railroads had been damaged or destroyed during the war, and much farmland was ravaged. The Civil War and the Industrial Revolution also brought an end to plantation culture in the state and the beginning of a slow shift away from agriculture. The state had to make the transition away from slavery, which had been banned in the United States during the war.

Federal troops remained in Virginia during Reconstruction, a period that lasted until 1870. Their presence was supposed to ensure that African Americans were given their rights, such as the right to vote and the right to own property. However, many white Virginians resented the soldiers and the newly freed African Americans. In the decades that followed Reconstruction, the state passed many laws that discriminated against African Americans. Many of these laws were not overturned until the 1960s.

The first part of the twentieth century was a difficult time for Virginians. Many of the state's African Americans fled widespread and harsh discrimination to look for jobs and better lives in the North. The

L. Douglas Wilder celebrates his victory in the 1989 gubernatorial election. He was the first African American to be elected governor in the history of the United States.

Great Depression brought a halt to the state's industries. Virginia began to recover during World War II, when thousands of new government jobs in the nation's capital brought more people into the state to live in Washington, D.C.'s suburbs in northern Virginia.

During the 1950s and 1960s, many of the state's discriminatory laws were struck down, including laws that segregated schools, prohibited people of different races from marrying, and required voters to pay a tax at the polls. In 1989, Virginia voters elected L. Douglas Wilder, an African American, as their governor. Wilder was the first African American to be elected governor in the United States.

Chapter 3

THE GOVERNMENT OF VIRGINIA

Virginia has long had close ties to the federal government. Eight presidents have come from the state, and many of the people who live in Washington, D.C.'s Virginia suburbs work for the federal government. Virginia's own government is one of the oldest in the United States.

Branches of Government

Like the federal government, the state government of Virginia is divided into three branches: the executive, legislative, and judicial. The executive branch, led by the governor, consists of a mix of elected and appointed officials.

The governor is the head of the executive branch. The governor serves as commander in chief of the state's police force and militia, enforces laws, and prepares the state budget. The governor also makes political appointments to statewide offices.

Virginia's legislative branch, called the State Assembly, is a direct descendant of the House of Burgesses founded by colonists in 1619. This makes it the oldest gathering of elected officials in the United States. The State Assembly is bicameral, meaning that it has two levels, or houses. The Senate is the smaller chamber and has forty members, while the House has one hundred members. Each member represents a different district of the state and is elected by the people who live in his or her district. The State Assembly makes and passes state laws, sets tax rates for citizens and corporations, and approves the state budget.

The judicial branch consists of the state's courts. The courts interpret the laws passed by the assembly

The Governor's Mansion in Richmond, Virginia, completed in 1813, is the oldest occupied governor's mansion in the United States.

and decide legal cases. The court system itself has several layers. The state Supreme Court is made up of seven justices elected to twelve-year terms by the General Assembly. Other courts include the Court of Appeals, thirty-one circuit courts located throughout the state, district courts, and juvenile and domestic relations courts.

Virginia and the Presidency

Virginia has produced more presidents than any other state in the country. Since the end of the Revolutionary War, eight men from Virginia have served as president. Four of the first five presidents were Virginians. George Washington was the country's first president, serving from 1789 to 1797. Washington largely defined the president's role as the country's leader. Washington's secretary of state, Thomas Jefferson, served as the third president, from 1801 to 1809. Jefferson

Voting for Almost 400 Years

The first elected legislative assembly in the New World was created in Virginia in 1619. It was called the House of Burgesses. In 1776, the legislature became the House of Delegates, the lower house of Virginia's General Assembly. Today, it has one hundred members elected for terms of two years. In honor of the original House of Burgesses, every other year, the Virginia General Assembly leaves the state capital of Richmond and meets for one day in the restored Capitol at Colonial Williamsburg. In 2006, the assembly held a special session at Jamestown to mark the four hundredth anniversary of the founding of the colony.

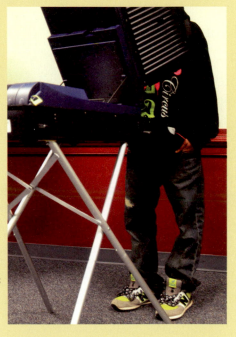

A voter casts his ballot on an electronic voting machine during the 2008 elections.

was immediately followed by two other Virginians—James Madison, who was president from 1809 to 1817, and James Monroe, who was president from 1817 to 1825.

Three other Virginians served as president during the nineteenth century. William Henry Harrison, famous for fighting the Battle of Tippecanoe against the Shawnee chief Tecumseh in 1811, took office

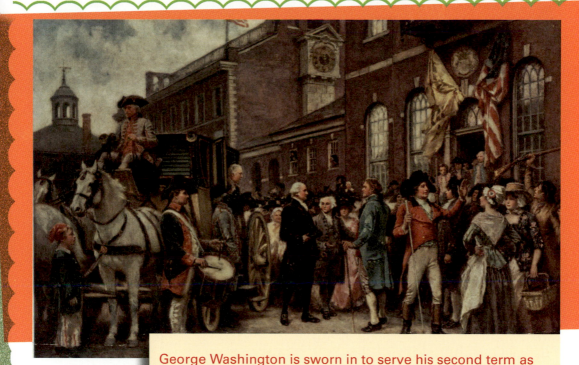

George Washington is sworn in to serve his second term as president in 1793. He declined to serve a third term, setting a precedent for future presidents.

as the ninth president in 1841. He died of a sudden illness just thirty days later. His vice president, another Virginian named John Tyler, became the first vice president to become president upon his predecessor's death. Zachary Taylor, a general during the Mexican-American War (1846–1848), became the twelfth president in 1849. Taylor also died while in office. Woodrow Wilson was the only Virginian elected president during the twentieth century. He served from 1913 to 1921, and guided the country through World War I.

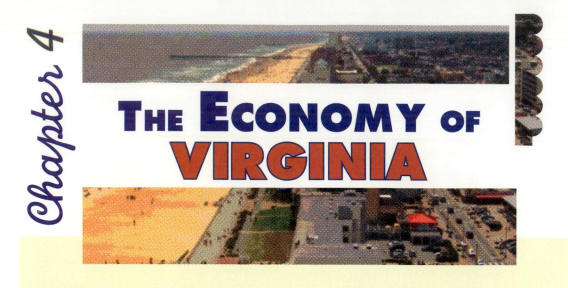

Chapter 4

THE ECONOMY OF VIRGINIA

Virginia's economic roots are in agriculture, dating back to the early days of the colony. Later, fishing, manufacturing, and mining also became important, though agriculture remained an economic mainstay. Today, however, high-tech jobs are spreading throughout the state, while travel and tourism grow as more people discover Virginia's rich history and scenic beauty.

Agriculture

Farming is a statewide industry in Virginia, even though agriculture brings in only about 1 percent of the state's annual income. Farms can be found from the flatlands of the Tidewater region to the mountainous west. On average, Virginia farms are relatively small, about 180 acres (0.73 sq km). Farming still brings in about $2.5 billion a year, placing it twenty-ninth in the nation in terms of agricultural output.

Tobacco became the first true cash crop in the North American colonies. Tobacco was native to the New World. Native Americans smoked the plant's leaves, a habit that quickly caught on in Europe. The tobacco that the Native Americans in Virginia cultivated, however, was harsh to European tastes. Colonist John Rolfe planted a milder species of tobacco plant using seeds from the Caribbean. The tobacco

28

A peanut farmer holds up some recently harvested peanut plants. Agriculture remains an economic mainstay in rural parts of the state, especially in the Piedmont region.

crop he sent to England in 1615 marked the first time the Jamestown colony turned a profit. The London investors who funded the colony offered land in the colony to Englishmen who were willing to go to Virginia and grow tobacco. The tempting offer provided a huge boost to Virginia, as more than four thousand Englishmen who wouldn't have been able to own land in England moved to the colony between 1619 and 1625. Tobacco remained the backbone of Virginia's economy for many years.

While tobacco was long the state's most important crop, Virginia's farms grew other products as well. The Tidewater region became a major source of fresh fruits and vegetables. Today, major crops grown in the state include potatoes, peanuts, and apples. The Piedmont region, in particular, is known as an apple-growing region. Farmers also raise livestock including cows, sheep, and pigs.

The Chesapeake Bay is one of the state's greatest economic assets. Commercial fishing has been an industry along the bay for centuries. The bay is particularly famous for its crabs, but fish and shellfish, such as oysters, are also an important part of the bay's fishing industry.

Manufacturing and Technology

Manufacturing didn't have a large presence in Virginia's economy until World War I, when factories across the country increased production to meet the military's demand for weapons and other supplies. It wasn't until then that the state's small manufacturing sector began recovering from the Civil War, when many factories were destroyed.

Today, there are many diverse industries across the state, and about 10 percent of the population works in manufacturing. Furniture and textile factories employ many people. Other important manufacturing sectors include chemicals, cigarettes, plastics, and paper products.

Shipbuilding and railroads are both major industries in the state. Today, the Newport News Shipbuilding and Dry Dock Company is the world's largest privately owned shipyard in the world. New ships are built and launched there, while others come into the docks for repairs. Norfolk Southern, a large freight railway corporation, employs thousands of people across the state. The Norfolk-based company ships goods across the country over thousands of miles of tracks.

Coal mining is a major industry in some parts of the Ridge and Valley region. As in neighboring West Virginia and Kentucky, the mountains of Virginia contain coal deposits. Many communities in the region rely on coal mining, even as environmentalists criticize mining practices like mountaintop removal. This is a practice in which mountains are literally stripped away in order to remove the coal more easily. Though coal mining declined steadily during the 1990s, high oil prices have renewed interest in coal, including finding cleaner ways to use it as a fuel.

Many people living in northern Virginia work for the federal government. The Pentagon, home to the Defense Department, is located in Virginia's Arlington County and employs twenty-three thousand people. Some work for other government departments in the capital or for companies that the government employs.

A nuclear-powered aircraft carrier is under construction in Newport News. The U.S. Navy has a large presence in Virginia.

The U.S. military is also a major employer in the state. The Norfolk Naval Base is the largest in the world. Apart from the U.S. Navy personnel who live and work on the base, thousands of civilians work to support its operation and supply its needs. The U.S. Army, Marines, Air Force, and Coast Guard also have important bases in the state.

In recent years, the Washington, D.C., suburbs in northern Virginia have become a vital center for the development of new technologies. More than one thousand computer communication companies are

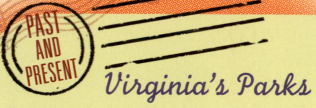

Virginia's Parks

Though once sites of nightmarish death, destruction, sorrow, and mourning, the many important Civil War battlefields that are found throughout Virginia have in recent decades become major tourist draws. Many of the state's Civil War battlefields, such as the sites of the battles of Manassas and Chancellorsville, are designated parks.

A new kind of destruction threatens this sacred ground now. Development in the northern part of the state is encroaching on battlefields that historians say should be protected. Virginia's tourism industry is boosted by its parklands. State and national parks can be found in every region, from the Assateague Island National Seashore in the Tidewater to Shenandoah National Park in the west.

based in northern Virginia. Cell phone companies also have a large presence in the state.

Tourism

Today, tourism accounts for an ever-growing portion of Virginia's economy. Tourism brings about $10 billion to the state every year. The state's long and rich history, as well as its varied and uniquely beautiful landscapes, draws millions of people to Virginia every year. People come to experience history brought to vivid life at meticulously restored Colonial Williamsburg and accurate recreations of Jamestown and neighboring Powhatan villages. They also tour the many Civil War battlefields scattered throughout the state.

Many tourists flock to Virginia to see historic sites. At some sites, such as Colonial Williamsburg, costumed actors bring history to life by playing the roles of colonial figures.

People come to Virginia to camp, hike, canoe, and fish. They may visit cultural destinations like Wolf Trap Farm Park for the Performing Arts, an outdoor venue near Washington known for its summer music festival. Others may see a play at the Barter Theater in rural Abingdon, designated the official state theater and renowned as a career launching pad for actors. Millions of people come to Richmond every year to see the city's monuments and museums.

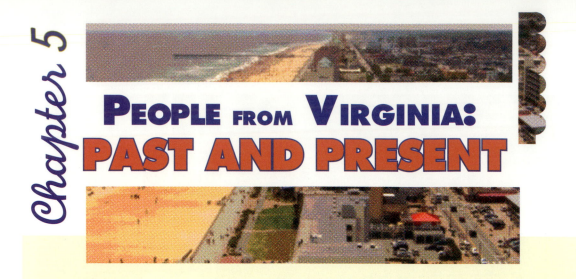

Chapter 5

PEOPLE FROM VIRGINIA: PAST AND PRESENT

Though not the most populous state in the country by a long shot, Virginia has produced a disproportionate number of luminaries, especially within the world of politics.

Politicians

Patrick Henry (1736–1799) Virginia's first state governor. Before the Revolutionary War, Patrick Henry was one of the most outspoken proponents of independence from England. He is best known for his famous "Give me liberty, or give me death" speech, made in Richmond in 1775.

Robert E. Lee (1807–1870) Robert E. Lee was an officer in the U.S. Army when the Civil War began in 1861. He resigned to become a general in the Confederate army and eventually commanded all Confederate forces. He became president of Washington College—later renamed Washington and Lee University—after the war ended.

James Madison (1751–1836) James Madison was the fourth president of the United States. He is often referred to as the "Father of the Constitution" for his role in writing that document and the Bill of Rights. Before being elected president in 1808, he was a member of the House of Representatives and secretary of state under Thomas Jefferson.

Woodrow Wilson (1856–1924) Woodrow Wilson was elected president in 1912, becoming the eighth Virginian to hold the office. His time in office was marked first by his efforts to keep the United States out of World War I, and then by the country's eventual involvement in the war beginning in 1917. Wilson helped shape the Treaty of Versailles, signed in 1919, which formally ended the war with Germany, one of the members of the Axis Powers that had fought the Allies.

Athletes and Entertainers

Arthur Ashe (1943–1993) Richmond-born Arthur Ashe became the first African American man to win the singles title at the Wimbledon tennis tournament in 1975. Ashe was accidentally infected with the HIV virus during a blood transfusion and spent the last years of his life working to raise funds for AIDS research.

Tennis great Arthur Ashe holds up his trophy after winning the 1975 Wimbledon Championship in England.

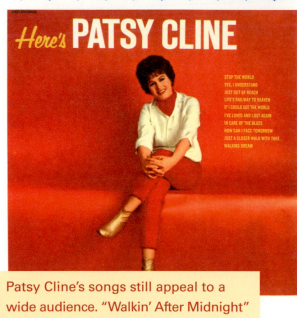

Here's **PATSY CLINE**

STOP THE WORLD
YES, I UNDERSTAND
JUST OUT OF REACH
LIFE'S RAILWAY TO HEAVEN
IF I COULD SEE THE WORLD
I'VE LOVED AND LOST AGAIN
IN CARE OF THE BLUES
HOW CAN I FACE TOMORROW
JUST A CLOSER WALK WITH THEE
WALKING DREAM

Patsy Cline's songs still appeal to a wide audience. "Walkin' After Midnight" and "I Fall to Pieces" were hits on country and pop charts.

June Carter Cash (1929–2003) June Carter Cash was a member of the famed country music group the Carter Family. She performed with family members on radio programs throughout the state, and they eventually became world-famous recording artists. She married country music star Johnny Cash in 1968. Though best known as a singer and musician, she also starred in movies and television shows.

Patsy Cline (1932–1963) Patsy Cline was a country music singer from Winchester. During her lifetime, she was famous for hits including "Crazy" and "I Fall to Pieces." Cline died in a plane crash in 1963 but remains a strong influence in country music today. She was elected to the Country Music Hall of Fame in 1973.

Ella Fitzgerald (1918–1996) Ella Fitzgerald was an award-winning jazz singer. Born in Newport News, she won fourteen

Ella Fitzgerald was known for her vocal range and ability to improvise. Her versions of songs by jazz composers Duke Ellington and Cole Porter are considered classics.

Grammy Awards for her recordings and performances over a career that spanned more than fifty years. She worked with such jazz greats as Louis Armstrong, Count Basie, and Duke Ellington.

Shirley MacLaine (1934–) Actress Shirley MacLaine was born in Richmond and became known for starring roles in films including *The Apartment*, *The Trouble with Harry*, and *Steel Magnolias*. In 1983, she won the Academy Award for

A Growing and Changing Population

The first colonists to arrive in Virginia, at Jamestown Island in 1607, numbered 103 and were all male. They were mostly farmers, sailors, and gentlemen adventurers and investors. Most were English, though a few were Dutch and Polish (hired from Prussia). The swampy, mosquito-ridden area offered few agricultural and hunting opportunities, and resulted in many deaths by disease and starvation. The Jamestown settlers were forced to wander farther afield for planting and foraging. Their efforts paid off. The Virginia Colony eventually expanded, thrived, and became one of the most powerful and influential of the thirteen original colonies, supported by a mighty plantation economy.

Today, Virginia boasts a population of more than seven million, composed of people with African, English, Scottish, Irish, German, Native American, Hispanic, and Asian ancestries, among others. A great number of Virginia's citizens work in the high-tech and Internet technology fields, the defense industry, agriculture, or for the federal government.

Best Actress for her role in *Terms of Endearment*. MacLaine has also authored several successful books.

Ralph Stanley (1927–) Ralph Stanley is one of the best-known bluegrass musicians in the world. He and his brother Carter Stanley formed the groundbreaking Clinch Mountain Boys in 1946, drawing heavily from traditional musical styles in writing their own songs. Stanley's work was prominently featured in the popular 2000 film *O Brother, Where Art Thou?*

and its top-selling soundtrack.

Writers

Edgar Allan Poe
(1809–1849) Poet and author Edgar Allan Poe grew up in Richmond. Though he did not become a successful writer during his lifetime, today he is considered a pioneering master of horror stories like "The Tell-Tale Heart" and detective stories like "The Murders in the Rue Morgue." Many of his poems, such as "The Raven" and "The Bells," are also widely known, read, studied, and enjoyed.

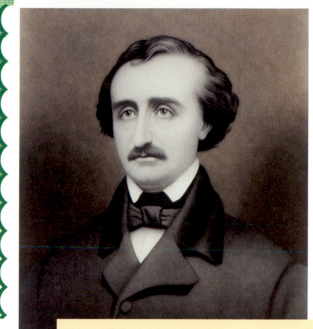

Writer Edgar Allen Poe was a master of the short story. Since his death in 1849, his tales have inspired generations of mystery and horror writers.

Tom Wolfe (1930–) Tom Wolfe is a renowned journalist and author who was born in Richmond. He was a pioneer of the "New Journalism" movement in the 1960s and 1970s, in which journalists inserted themselves into the situations that they were documenting. Wolfe's nonfiction work includes *The Right Stuff*, while his best-known novel is *Bonfire of the Vanities*.

Timeline

1607	Settlers from England establish the colony of Jamestown.
1619	The House of Burgesses is established; the first Africans are brought to Virginia as indentured servants.
1676	Nathaniel Bacon leads a rebellion against Virginia's colonial government.
1775	George Washington becomes commander in chief of the Continental army.
1776	Thomas Jefferson writes the Declaration of Independence.
1780	Richmond becomes Virginia's capital.
1781	General Washington's Continental army wins the Battle of Yorktown, the last major conflict of the Revolutionary War.
1787	Virginian James Madison writes the U.S. Constitution and the Bill of Rights.
1788	Virginia becomes the tenth state to ratify the Constitution.
1789	George Washington is elected the first president of the United States.
1819	Thomas Jefferson founds the University of Virginia.
1859	Abolitionist John Brown leads a raid against the arsenal at Harpers Ferry.
1861	Virginia secedes from the Union to join the Confederate States of America.
1865	Confederate general Robert E. Lee surrenders at Appomattox Courthouse.
1870	Reconstruction ends in Virginia, and the state rejoins the Union.
1912	Virginian Woodrow Wilson is elected president of the United States.
1959	Virginia schools begin desegregating.
1989	L. Douglas Wilder becomes the first African American elected governor in the United States.
2007	Virginia celebrates the four hundredth anniversary of Jamestown's founding.
2008	Virginia votes for a Democratic presidential candidate, Barack Obama, who would go on to become the first African American president of the United States. This was the first time that Virginia voted for a Democratic presidential candidate since the majority of state residents voted for Lyndon B. Johnson in 1964.

State motto	*Sic Semper Tyrannis* ("Thus Always to Tyrants")
State capital	Richmond
State flag	Virginia's state flag shows the state seal on a field of blue. It was first used in the 1830s but was not formally adopted until 1930.
State seal	Virginia's state seal shows the goddess of virtue holding a spear in her right hand and a sheathed sword in her left hand. Her left foot rests on the chest of a figure representing tyranny. Above the figure is the word "Virginia," and the state motto appears underneath the figure. The seal was designed by Virginian George Wythe and was adopted in 1776.
State flower	Flowering dogwood
State bird	Cardinal
State tree	Flowering dogwood
Statehood date and number	June 25, 1788, tenth state
State nicknames	"Old Dominion," "Mother of States," "Mother of Presidents"
Total area and U.S. rank	42,328 square miles (109,629 sq km), thirty-fifth largest state
Population	7,078,515
Length of coastline	112 miles (180 kilometers)

State Flag

State Seal

Highest elevation	Mount Rogers, at 5,729 feet (1,746 m)
Lowest elevation	Sea level, at the Atlantic Ocean
Major rivers	Appomattox, Clinch, Dan, Elizabeth, Holston, James, New, North Anna, Nottoway, Potomac, Rappahannock, Roanoke, Shenandoah, South Anna, York
Major lakes	Lake Anna, Buggs Island Lake, Claytor Lake, Lake Drummond, Lake Gaston, Mountain Lake, Smith Mountain Lake, South Holston Lake
Hottest temperature recorded	110°F (43°C), at Balcony Falls, July 15, 1954
Coldest temperature recorded	-30°F (-34°C), at Mountain Lake Biological Station, January 25, 1985
Origin of state name	Virginia was named in honor of England's Queen Elizabeth I, who never married and was thus nicknamed "the Virgin Queen"
Chief agricultural products	Tobacco, apples, poultry, cattle, hogs, soybeans, corn, wheat, hay
Major industries	Manufacturing, exports, agriculture, tourism, mining, general services, transportation, communication and utilities, finance, insurance, real estate, technology, government

State Bird

State Flower

abolish To do away with or end.

agriculture The science, art, and business of cultivating the soil and raising crops and livestock.

bicameral Having two branches, houses, or chambers, as a legislative body.

charter A written grant of specified rights made by a government or ruler to an individual, group, or corporation.

civilian A person who is not on active duty with a military, naval, police, or firefighting organization.

colony Any people or territory separated from a home country but subject to the rules of its government.

district A division of territory, as of a country, state, or county, marked off for administrative, electoral, or other purposes.

domesticated Tamed and bred for use by humans.

estuary Part of the mouth or lower course of a river, where the river's current meets the sea's tide.

indentured servant A person who is bonded or contracted to work for another for a specified period of time in exchange for learning a trade or paying a debt.

neck A narrow, projecting strip of land.

peninsula Land that is almost entirely surrounded by water and connected with the mainland by an isthmus (a narrow strip of land with water on two sides and land on either end).

plateau A land area having a relatively level surface that is considerably raised above adjoining land on at least one side.

ratify To approve and make valid.

Reconstruction In the post–Civil War years, the process by which the Southern states that had seceded were readmitted into the Union.

secede To formally withdraw from membership in or association with a group, federation, or organization.

segregation The policy and practice of separating people of different races, classes, or ethnic groups, especially as a form of discrimination.

Colonial Williamsburg Foundation

P.O. Box 1776

Williamsburg, VA 23187

(757) 229-1000

Web site: http://www.history.org

The Colonial Williamsburg Foundation operates the living history museum in Williamsburg.

Mariners' Museum

100 Museum Drive

Newport News, VA 23606

(757) 596-2222

Web site: http://www.mariner.org

The Mariners' Museum in Newport News is one of the largest maritime museums in the world.

Shenandoah National Park

3655 Highway 211 East

Luray, VA 22835

(540) 999-3601

Web site: http://www.nps.gov/shen/index.htm

Shenandoah National Park covers a significant portion of the Shenandoah Valley, preserving both the region's history and its natural beauty.

U.S. National Slavery Museum

1320 Central Park Boulevard, Suite 251

Fredericksburg, VA 22401

(540) 548-8818

Web site: http://www.usnationalslaverymuseum.org

The U.S. National Slavery Museum is envisioned as a means to educate the public about slavery and to commemorate the struggle for freedom.

Virginia Department of Historic Resources

2801 Kensington Avenue

Richmond, VA 23221

(804) 367-2323

Web site: http://www.dhr.virginia.gov

The Virginia Department of Historic Resources is the state's historic preservation office.

Virginia Historical Society

P.O. Box 7311

Richmond, VA 23221

(804) 358-4901

Web site: http://www.vahistorical.org

The Virginia Historical Society is dedicated to preserving the state's past.

Web Sites

Due to the changing nature of Internet links, Rosen Publishing has developed an online list of Web sites related to the subject of this book. This site is updated regularly. Please use this link to access this list:

http://www.rosenlinks.com/uspp/vapp

FOR FURTHER READING

Arnold, James A. *The Civil War*. Minneapolis, MN: Lerner Publications, 2005.

Barrett, Tracy. *Celebrate the States: Virginia*. New York, NY: Benchmark, 2006.

Fradin, Dennis. *Jamestown, Virginia*. New York, NY: Benchmark, 2007.

Henry, Marguerite. *Misty of Chincoteague*. New York, NY: Aladdin, 2006.

O'Connell, Kim. *Virginia*. Berkeley Heights, NJ: Enslow Publishing, 2003.

Pobst, Sandy. *Life in the 13 Colonies: Virginia*. New York, NY: Children's Press, 2004.

Rudolph, Ellen K. *Willie Gets a History Lesson in Virginia's Historic Triangle*.Walland, TN: EKR Publications, 2007.

Whitcraft, Melissa. *The Surrender at Yorktown*. New York, NY: Children's Press, 2004.

BIBLIOGRAPHY

Craven, Wesley Frank. *White, Red, and Black: The Seventeenth-Century Virginian*. New York, NY: W. W. Norton and Company, 1971.

Kelley, C. Brian. *Best Little Stories from Virginia*. Nashville, TN: Cumberland House, 2003.

Mark, Rebecca, and Rob Vaughn, eds. *The South*. Westport, CT: Greenwood Press, 2004.

McGraw, Marie Tyler. *At the Falls: Richmond, Virginia, & Its People*. Chapel Hill, NC: The University of North Carolina Press, 1994.

Mock, Greg, and Tom Dietrich. *Virginia's Shenandoah Valley*. Helena, MT: American Geographic Publishing, 1990.

Smith, Julian. *Virginia*. Emeryville, CA: Avalon Travel Publishing, 2005.

Trefler, Caroline, ed. *Fodor's Virginia and Maryland*. New York, NY: Random House, 2007.

Virginia Legislative Office. *Factpack: Facts About the Commonwealth of Virginia*. Richmond, VA: Virginia Tourism Corporation, 2007.

Virginia Writers' Project. *Virginia: A Guide to the Old Dominion*. New York, NY: Oxford University Press, 1941.

INDEX

About the Author

Jason Porterfield has written numerous books for Rosen on many aspects of American history. A native Virginian, Porterfield graduated from Oberlin College in 2001 with a B.A. in English, history, and religion. In 2008, he earned an M.A. in journalism from Columbia College, Chicago. He currently lives in Chicago.

Photo Credits

Cover (top, left) MPI/Getty Images; cover (top, right), p. 31 Courtesy of Northrop Grumman/U.S. Navy; cover (bottom), pp. 3, 6, 15, 20, 24, 28, 34, 40, 41 (right), 42 Wikimedia Commons; p. 4 (top) © GeoAtlas; p. 8 Skip Brown/National Geographic/Getty Images; p. 10 © Marc Muench/Corbis; p. 12 © www.istockphoto.com/catnap72; pp. 13, 29 © Karen Kasmauski/Corbis; p. 16 © Marilyn Angel Wynn/Nativestock Pictures/Corbis; p. 17 The Stapleton Collection/Art Resource, NY; pp. 18, 22, 27, 39 Library of Congress Prints and Photographs Division; p. 23 © Bettmann/Corbis; p. 25 © www.istockphoto.com/Bill Manning; p. 26 Karen Bleier/AFP/Getty Images; p. 33 http://www.colonialwilliamsburg.com; p. 35 Focus on Sports/Getty Images; p. 36 Michael Ochs Archives/Getty Images; p. 37 Yale Joel/Time & Life Pictures/Getty Images; p. 41 (left) Courtesy of Robesus, Inc.

Designer: Les Kanturek; Photo Researcher: Amy Feinberg